authentic faith

fresh expressions of church amongst young adults

fresh expressions

What is a fresh expression of church?

A **fresh expression** is a form of church for our changing culture, established primarily for the benefit of people who are not yet members of any church.

It will come into being through principles of listening, service, incarnational mission and making disciples.

It will have the potential to become a mature expression of church shaped by the gospel and the enduring marks of the church and for its cultural context.

Fresh expressions of church:

- **serve those outside church;**
- **listen to people and enter their culture;**
- **make discipleship a priority;**
- **form church.**

The **Fresh Expressions** organisation exists to encourage and resource these new ways of being church, working with Christians from a broad range of denominations and traditions. The movement has resulted in thousands of new congregations being formed alongside more traditional churches.

Contents

Introduction

	References
1.	**Churchgoing in the UK** Ian Farthing, Tearfund, 2007, p15
2.	**Pulling out of the nosedive: A contemporary Picture of Churchgoing: What the 2005 English Church Census Reveals** Peter Brierley, Christian Research, 2006, p116

The Church is failing to reach or keep young adults. Only 11% of regular churchgoers are between the ages of 25 and 34, whilst 16% of the population is within that age group [1]. In tracking decline, the greatest losses per year are occurring amongst those aged 15 to 29 [2]. However, there are churches bucking this trend.

This report outlines the findings from a qualitative research project undertaken by Church Army and Fresh Expressions looking into some of these churches including: parish churches, traditional church plants and fresh expressions of church all with growing numbers of people in their 20s and 30s.

This research provides evidence that some larger churches, with young adult congregations, that are contemporary in style yet with more traditional practices, such as Sunday services alongside midweek groups, are effectively reaching middle class, well educated young adults, who previously attended church as children.

However, the churches managing to reach young adults with no prior faith or church experience, and from a broader socio-economic background, exhibit very different traits and practices.

This study examines the emerging Christian practices amongst young adults and how church is being rediscovered by those growing Christian communities among those beyond the fringes of church.

This report outlines the background issues associated with research into this age group, the research model employed, commonality and difference between practices, the existence of five types of young adult church, conclusions and the following recommendations.

Recommendations

1 There is evidence of five distinct types of young adults' church. These types each connect with different kinds of young adults and practice their faith differently. These different dynamics should be recognised, understood and encouraged by the wider Church.

2 The churches reaching closed de-churched and non-churched young adults develop community practices more often around the dining table than the church building. Access to communal spaces, such as provided by larger vicarages or manses, can make a crucial difference to the growth and sustainability of these Christian communities.

3 The rise of small sacramental communities needs further understanding. Issues remain about permissions, authorisation, and the appropriate administration of the sacraments, which need careful consideration. Some dioceses, and some acknowledged mission communities, are making strides in recognising, endorsing and supporting these types of churches.

4 Churches reaching young adults with no prior experience of church, or who have rejected church with no intention of returning, are developing more experimental forms of Christian community. These churches are greatly affected by the level of support and connection with the wider church. However, their unconventional style can be a stumbling block to this. More can and should be done to encourage open and supportive connections between the wider church and these fledgling communities.

Church planting hubs act as gathering points, and are highly effective in attracting, retaining and discipling young adults with childhood church experience and faith. These churches should be valued by the wider church in the important role they play in retaining young adults as they transition out of churches they attended as children. These hub churches have a crucial role in preparing young adults for a vocational life of mission in the world and ministry in the church.

Those starting fresh expressions of church for young people should make provision in time for the subsequent development of a young adult church, especially when working with young people unlikely to move away from home to go to university.

Many dioceses have specialists acting as children's work advisors and diocesan youth officers. Arguably there is an even greater need in work with young adults. Posts should be created both to help multiple new churches to form and to support existing young adult churches. This work would include:

- finding sustainable patterns of leadership;
- affirming areas of good practice;
- support through periods of transition;
- guidance towards a contextual sacramental life;
- building positive relationships with the wider Church;
- guidance on development over time as the young adults grow up.

5

6

7

Background issues

Young adult movement

There is currently an uneven distribution of young adult involvement in all types of church, traditional church plants and fresh expressions of church. An extremely high proportion of young adults in church are found in London churches [3], followed by churches in university cities. Much fewer exist in rural and Urban Priority Areas (UPAs). This trend highlights the wider movement of young adults moving out of home and into cities for university and jobs. This represents a year by year influx of Christian young adults, looking for, or open to becoming part of a church.

Whilst churches in these areas are right to attend to this reality and both traditional church and fresh expressions of church can respond to this, it would be naïve to ignore the wider trend of the movement among young adults. A church in one of these locations may grow year on year and have a thriving young adult ministry, with only a minimal growth of new Christians and significant numbers of young adults leaving.

Sociological development

Whilst young adults may be marrying and having children at a later age, this remains the key time when young adults socialise within their own peer group - they date and look for partnerships. The implication is that a church with young

3. **Pulling out of the nosedive: A contemporary Picture of Churchgoing: What the 2005 English Church Census Reveals**
Peter Brierley, Christian Research, 2006, p116

adults is attractive to other young adults, and conversely being the only young adult (or one of a few) plays against this group's sociological drives.

Different streams of young adults

Whilst many young adults do move for university or work, many others remain in their home cities, towns and in rural areas. Young adults remaining at or near home often come from more deprived areas. Any research of mission among young adults would need to take account of this.

A model of research which simplistically tracks large young adult ministries in university locations will be skewed to a particular section of society.

Implications

Given these three factors we would expect to see larger young adult involvement in churches in cities that are located near universities and that become hubs for Christian young adults. These churches are well placed to attract other young adults who are interested in Christianity. They can also become a training ground for Christian young leaders, and will benefit from the time and resources of the large numbers of young adults contributing to the ministry and mission of the church.

A number of churches have become significant young adult hubs and there is much to learn from the ministries and fresh expressions of Church that have developed there. However, young adult movement and the sociological drives of the age groups have played an important factor in this. In identifying 'successful' ministries, existence of these phenomena must be clear. Numbers attending can not simply be translated as 'success' without taking into account the underlying trends and the types of young adults that are present. Nor can a single model of church for young adults be expected to work in contexts where other dynamics are in play.

The research model

This small scale qualitative research project takes a grounded theory approach, with theoretical sampling to examine the emerging practices amongst churches with growing numbers of young adults. It was clear at the outset that any such study could not simplistically look at churches with large numbers of young adults but instead needed to track the types of young adults attending, both in terms of their socio-economic background and their religious background as children and teens.

The scope of the research was not to identify churches with young adults present amongst all ages; rather, this research looked at churches with growing numbers of young adults. This included parish churches with young adult congregations, traditional church plants, fresh expressions of church, and some examples of Christian ministry amongst young adults which may, or may not, yet be church.

4. **Encounters on the Edge, 30**
George Lings, The Sheffield Centre,
Church Army, 2006, pp16-20

References

There was much debate on the definition of 'young adult'. A conventional definition of young adult, as those having left university but not yet embarked on family life and the arrival of children, could be used. However, this defines not just the age group but a certain demographic of young adult, which excludes the large numbers of young adults who do not go on to higher education. Instead, for the purposes of this study, the term young adult refers to people between the ages of 20 and 35 years. Whilst attendees were not discounted as young adults for being students or having children, churches which were focused either on students (campus based or existing primarily for students) or on young families were discounted.

Theoretical sampling was employed to identify twelve representative churches. Details of the churches involved can be found at the end of the report. The range of churches identified covers those reaching young adults from a breadth of socio-economic and religious backgrounds, based in locations across the country. However, no rural examples were found, so all the churches examined are located in towns or cities. Also a range of ecclesial tradition was difficult to find and this is discussed later.

One apostolic mandate is given in Acts 1.8: 'When the Spirit comes, you will be my witnesses in Jerusalem, Judea, Samaria and the ends of the earth'. This has been applied to a journey from mission to the familiar and open (fringe and open de-churched), through the disagreeable (closed de-church), to the unthinkable (non-churched) [4].

5. **Mission Shaped Evangelism**
Steve Hollinghurst, SCM Canterbury
Press, 2010, pp10-15

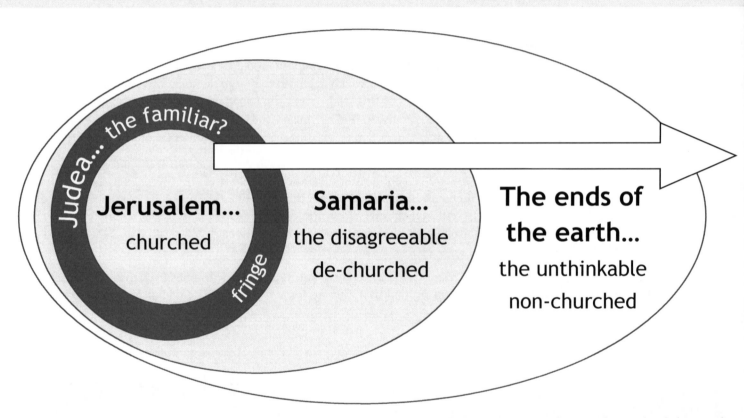

Diagram 1: Jerusalem to the ends of the earth

Mission and evangelism in the UK has tended to focus on 'Jerusalem and Judea', representing mission to fringe and open de-churched people. However, as the percentage of fringe and open dechurched people in the UK drops with each generation, this connects with a reducing minority of people [5]. So the vast majority of mission is done in a shrinking pond. This is increasingly important as younger generations show higher percentages of people with no experience of church. In identifying growing young adult churches, care was taken in identifying whether these relate to the categories Jerusalem and Judea, Samaria or ends of the earth (diagram 2). Lessons learnt from these different contexts can then more accurately inform practice.

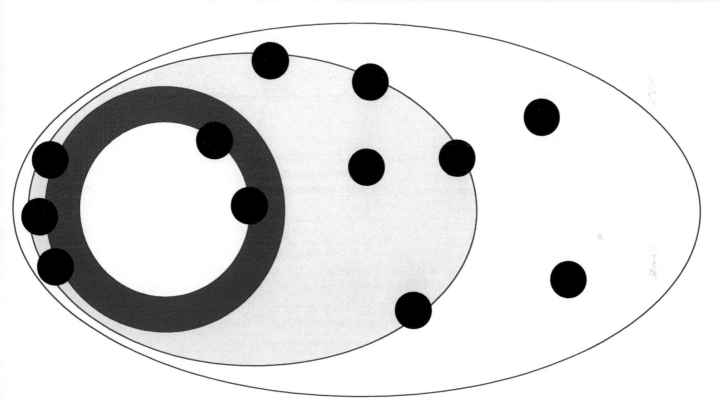

Diagram 2: The spread of churches examined on the Jerusalem to the ends of the earth spectrum

Semi-structured interviews were conducted over the phone, with leaders telling the story of how the church had started and developed. They were asked how and why they thought they had grown and were asked to describe who came along.

After a number of open ended questions, interviewees were asked to give more detailed accounts of growth, size and the types of people coming along, including their religious background. Alongside this, other details such as church affiliation and geographical location were collected.

Realities shared in common

There are a number of common values and realities seen across all or most churches involved in the study. These realities shaped their practice, their faith and how the community organised themselves. Whilst these realties were outworked in different ways, which will be discussed later, their presence across all or most of the expressions of church investigated suggests a commonality across ministries with this age group.

Community

Community was a key value within the churches. Food, socials, hospitality were all key components of church life rather than additional activities. The term family was used frequently, particularly in reference to church as family, both for those from broken family backgrounds, or a family away from home for those having recently moved away from their parents' home for university or jobs.

Authenticity

Honesty, integrity, and 'realness' were emphasised over 'rightness'. Church was described as journeying together, working out faith, together, in the messy realities of life, rather than the teaching of truths. Leadership was defined by honesty and in connecting with others in their struggles, rather than being detached or idealist about faith. Discipleship was described as working out how to do life well, rather than how to believe the right things.

Doubt

Across most of the churches value was placed on an openness to express doubt, to question, to deconstruct. This was often understood as a valuable formational phase in the church's life, enabling members to develop and own its vision and ethos. Churches reaching people with no previous church experience or closed de-churched young adults allowed more freedom in this area, with some leaders describing discipleship as moving through doubt towards faith. Some leaders found the presence of such high levels of doubt hampered the growth of their church. Leaders of churches reaching churched young adults also valued the space to express doubt and questions, but members of these churches had less freedom to question and a quicker expectation on them to move beyond doubt. This resulted in a number of young adults leaving, but allowed a more positive Christian community to develop amongst those who remained.

Spirituality

Most of the leaders interviewed, across the range of churches, emphasised the emotive or 'felt' nature of a spiritual encounter with God. Creative and experiential worship during church services was rated as a high value for young adults with previous church experience. For churches reaching closed de-churched or non-churched the term worship was not used, but rather 'spaces' where people could experience God. These spaces often looked very different from the sung worship happening within a traditional church service environment.

Change

All the leaders interviewed discussed how change was an ongoing reality of their church. They described a continuous transition of people in and out of the community. This was caused by people moving geographically, for work, study, and resettlement. Transition was also caused by people moving to a new life stage. These ongoing transitions affected members and leaders and had a significant impact on the development of the church. Larger churches emphasised the need for robust and supportive structures to balance the negative effects of transition. Smaller churches emphasised the strength of relationship and the important role the wider church can play, especially during leadership transitions.

In practice

Whilst there is evidence of commonality across the churches examined, these realities of community, authenticity, doubt, spirituality and change were worked out in very different practices. Though these realities shaped their faith and practice, there were noticeable differences between the types of churches, their contexts and the kinds of young adults reached.

Five types

Five distinct types of young adults' church were identified during this study. Initially these were identified by the sorts of questions that appeared to have defined and shaped how and why the church started, how they grew and how they described the story of their development. It became clear through further analysis of the transcripts that this typology extended and was confirmed by a number of other factors such as size, practices, sacramental practice, buildings used and context. Below is a summary of the five types, which are then described in more detail.

Type	Defining questions	Reaching	Size	Context
1. Church planting hubs	How do we retain and attract more young adults?	Christian and open de-churched	100+	Middle class well educated. In or near student areas
2. Youth church grown up	How do we grow up into adult church for us?	Young adult growth: Christians and open de-churched	100+	Middle class well educated even where teen context was different
3. De-constructed church	What is Church?	Closed de-churched and non-churched	20-40, plus 50-100 in wider network	Middle class, highly educated and vulnerable people
4. Church on the margins	What is gospel transformation for the poor?	Non-churched	12-30	UPAs, high levels of poverty, mental health problems, addictions, homelessness, criminal activity
5. Context shaped church	What is Church in this context?	Churched and non-churched	30, plus 100+ in wider network	Varies, and people excluded from church

Continued on next page...

Type	Sacraments	Practice	Buildings
1. Church planting hubs	As part of Sunday service, administered by authorised clergy	Sunday service plus midweek discipleship and mission	Church, homes, limited use of public space
2. Youth church grown up	As part of Sunday service, administered by authorised clergy	Sunday service plus midweek discipleship and mission	Church, homes, limited use of public space
3. De-constructed church	Around the table, often agape in style	Meet around a meal or for a project or task	Community homes, limited use of church buildings
4. Church on the margins	Agape style if at all	Discipleship, coaching, meals	Public spaces, homes
5. Context shaped church	Developed in context and administered by authorised clergy	Teaching, worship, prayer, discipleship birthed in context	Mixing sacred and secular spaces

1. Church planting hubs

What are they like?

Churches identifies as planting hubs were defined by questions on how to retain, disciple and attract more young adults.

They are contemporary in style, and with a specific service or congregation for young adults.

The church life is organised around a Sunday service alongside other community based activities. The Sunday service, which takes place in a traditional or new church building, includes sung worship, preaching, and sacraments are administered by authorised clergy.

The young adults meet midweek, in small groups, for discipleship and fellowship. These groups include a strong emphasis on mission and evangelism, through shared missional activities and personal witness.

Some of these churches run year out discipleship courses which feed into the life of the church, both attracting people from across the country and facilitating intensive discipleship opportunities for existing members.

Leaders described their churches as developing community, worship and evangelism. However, they noted that mission and evangelism were less developed than community and worship.

Who are they reaching?

These churches have large numbers of people in their 20s and 30s, with their young adult congregation having at least 100 people. They tend to largely reach young adults with a Christian upbringing, for example those moving into the area for work or study and looking for a church, or those returning to faith after a brief lapse at university. It was estimated that 80%-90% of those attending these churches had gone to church as children or teens. Leaders cited attractive worship, real and welcoming community, young adults in leadership and having a critical mass of young adults, as the reasons for their growth.

They are located in student and postgraduate areas, or in locations which are easily accessible and networked into that demographic. With that context it is then not surprising that they tend to reach middle class, well educated young adults.

What do they do?

Although these young adult congregations have their own services and small groups they are part of a larger church body. This enables the young adults to develop a young adults' church with the support and resource of the larger church.

These young adult churches benefit from the resource of buildings, church governance and accountability and leadership development. In some cases, churches also provided older wiser Christians to come alongside the young adults, especially when more demanding pastoral issues arose. This level of connection enables supportive, discipling and accountable structures to release inexperienced young adults into leadership.

"Invest in leaders, that's how you grow.

The oversight of clergy, working closely with lay leaders within these churches, ensures the sacraments can be administered regularly and enables connection with the wider Church.

Each of the churches researched were from a broadly charismatic evangelical tradition. They each had a similar structure: large supportive church, young adult congregation, small groups alongside social and missional activities. However, they also emphasised the importance of not copying other churches and avoiding the temptation to follow a set model or programme of church.

Each noted the significance of growing church within their context, and the place of ongoing discernment in the growth of the church.

Discipleship and leadership

These churches put a strong emphasis in discipling and releasing young adults into leadership. Young adults are involved in leading midweek groups and Sunday services. They also give young adults responsibility in making decisions for the groups and in pastoral care.

The intentional development of young adults, the support of the larger church body and the types of young adults they attract (middle class, well educated, Christian background) results in a steady flow of competent members with the time and resources to build up the church community and mission. The growth of leaders encourages the growth of more small groups and mission activities, attracting more members, with a supply of additional leaders to facilitate further small groups for rising numbers.

> " *Always build something that's scalable, then it can be reproduced and replicated easily.*

Multiplication

The churches interviewed in this type were involved in various forms of church multiplication. The language of traditional church plant and graft were used, as was the language of clusters and missional communities. These churches' ability to attract large numbers of Christian young adults makes them well placed to engage in church planting, either sending out larger groups of people to start church in a different location, or sending out multiple smaller groups to start developing fresh expressions of church.

Each of these churches had gained wisdom from being part of a planting process, recognising the effects on a congregation when significant numbers of core members are sent out to plant something new. Some of these churches had experienced quite large fluctuations of numbers and quite rapid changes when planting occurred. Numbers grew back up quickly, mainly through transfer growth and influx of students. However, leaders emphasised the pastoral impact of these changes.

Growth

Leaders of these churches noted a lack of resources as hampering their growth. None of these churches had a full time member of staff employed to focus solely on young adults. Given that the young adult congregations were between 100-250 people, they felt that staff resourcing was scarce.

They also highlighted that succession issues hampered the churches' growth, which happened when curates moved on, or when leaders moved out, with the further church being planted.

2. Youth church grown up

What are they like?

As the title suggests, these churches began life as youth ministries or youth churches. Ten years on, with members growing up and out of the youth church, but not connecting to other expressions of church, they began considering how their church could become a place for young adults.

In the churches researched here, it happened that both examples of youth church that grew up also fitted into the church planting hubs typology. So in these cases many of the aspects of the church planting hubs apply here, although their history is markedly different.

Rather than repeating the aspects found in common with church planting hubs, this section outlines the differences between these two types, which are in the main due to their differing historical mandates. However, it should be made clear that although the examples given in this research outline how these youth churches developed into church planting hubs, it does not follow that all youth churches will or should follow this pattern.

A few examples of youth churches growing up, which did not follow this pattern, were evident in the initial stages of this research but were discounted, as it was felt they were too early on in their development, for example Sorted, in Bradford. Future research into this will provide a more accurate picture of how youth churches are developing and growing up.

The youth churches in this study were asking similar questions to the church planting hubs: how do we retain, disciple and attract more young adults? However, when these youth churches began, the questions which defined how they developed and who they reached were more intentionally missional and contextual than the church planting hubs.

> **"It's not about fixing a smile on your face, it's about being authentic and real about the struggles whilst acknowledging that God is good.**

Who are they reaching?

In one example, a fresh expression grew almost exclusively amongst non-churched teenagers. In the other, a youth church was developed from a parish church, including the church's existing teenagers and others from the local school. This developed with about half non-churched teenagers and half from families at the church. So, proportionally, we see these churches reaching many more young adults from families who did not attend church. However, both leaders describing the young adult congregations which had developed out of youth churches, explained that whilst historical growth (as a youth church) had reached non-churched teenagers, growth amongst young adults was almost all from Christians transferring from other churches, or from students and postgraduates moving into the area, and so they were now reaching mainly churched, middle class and well educated young adults.

Difficulties were encountered when young people who had come to faith through the youth church did not fit with the developing demographic (either religious or socio-economic) of the young adult congregation. Sadly one church, a church planting hub with a previously thriving youth church, had lost many young people from non-churched and deprived backgrounds because they had been unable to transition from the youth church to the existing young adults' church. The two examples in this research of youth church grown up had successfully navigated this transition by growing the church up, developing additional young adult groups and congregations, rather than transferring people between very different congregations.

It is surprising that both youth churches studied, who had reached high proportions of non-churched teenagers and retained these as they grew into young adults, had almost exclusively gone on to only reach more young adults from Christian families. This raises questions about differences in reaching teens and young adults and highlights the difficulties encountered in reaching young adults with no previous church background.

"It's about being church, not doing church.

3. Deconstructed church

What are they like?

These churches were defined and shaped by questions such as 'what is church?'

They tended to be influenced by Christians who had previous church experience and did not want to go back (closed de-churched).

These Christian communities enabled members to question and practice their faith. Whilst all types emphasised the place of questioning, these churches were shaped by their willingness to dismantle what church is, in order to find authenticity.

What do they do?

Deconstructed churches do meet regularly but without the normal Sunday service features. They do not necessarily meet on Sunday, and probably not in a church building. There is no singing, and often no plan, or set service.

They meet around a specific task or project, or around the table. These churches placed a high value on community, with church practices based around meals. Prayer, thanksgiving and discipleship happen during the meal in which Communion is also shared.

With such an emphasis on community life, large enough communal spaces, either in vicarages or shared houses is key. When a vicarage was either provided, or lost, it impacted on the community's ability to grow or struggle to survive. There were examples of young adults living together in mission communities with some connections to new monasticism made. They also used sacred spaces for spiritual events. This worked well when a cathedral or town centre church allowed them to use their building. One of the

"Food is the new Sunday service.

communities studied was more reflective and emphasised worship alongside community. However, the other two were more activist in style, emphasising mission and community over worship.

From the churches studied, deconstructed churches were more likely than other types, although not exclusively, to have started by accident, rather than a diocesan initiative or from an existing church. Of all the types, deconstructed churches were least likely to be connected to the wider church. Whilst they lacked the resource of the wider church, they often found it less of a problem than context shaped churches or those on the margins.

Discipleship and leadership

Whilst there were often recognised leaders, they developed a flat leadership style, with decision making being more democratic. Leaders noted that this was the most appropriate leadership style, enabling members to take ownership of the group and get involved. However, it could result in drawn-out decision making and slow progress.

With ongoing transition, these churches struggled when key members of the community moved on. Succession issues, especially when leaders or core members moved on were hard to navigate, especially if this coincided with the loss of the community's home. To lose the leader and the building in one move was difficult.

Deconstructed churches were less likely to seek or gain permission and recognition from wider church structures. Some encountered issues with the wider church, others were not noticed by the wider church. The one example which was started as a Diocesan initiative appreciated close links with the Diocese and Cathedral. These links ensured its survival during a challenging transition period.

The deconstructed churches in this study have a small and transient community of 20-40 people, experiencing considerable transfer of people in and out. These churches also have a larger, and sometimes highly active, wider network of people connecting with activities organised through the church. These other activities and projects connect with people from a much broader socio-economic and religious background and, in particular, vulnerable young adults.

Who are they reaching?

The deconstructed churches studied were reaching a mix of closed de-churched and non-churched people.

In one church, about half were from a Christian background, of which many were closed de-churched and half with no previous church experience.

In another church 80% were classed as closed de-churched and 20% non-churched.

The third deconstructed church was 20% closed de-churched, 20% non-churched, 30% churched. They also identified 30% of their group growing up with a mixed faith background, where one parent was Christian and the other actively atheist or of another faith.

These deconstructed churches were reaching middle class, highly educated young adults and vulnerable young adults through project work.

Growth

Leaders cited evangelism, advertising, inviting people along, being good networkers, not having a church service, and developing opportunities for people to encounter God as factors in their growth. These also talked about how they had learnt through experience and the ongoing development of practices.

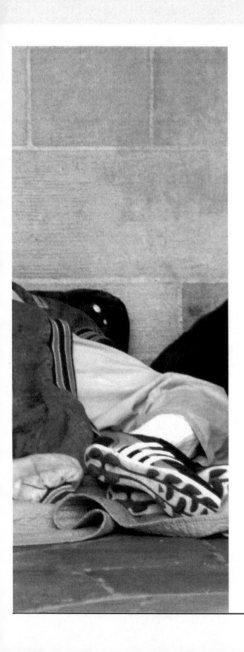

4. Church on the margins

What are they like?

Two of the churches studied were reaching young adults marginalised by wider society. These churches were developing within a specific context, so could have been identified as context shaped churches. However, they were being shaped by issues associated with deprivation and poverty, and raising questions more defined by levels of deprivation than age group context, such as 'What is the gospel for the poor?' and 'What does church look like among the marginalised?'

What do they do?

The focus here is on transforming the lives of the young adults; discipling people beyond exclusion, rather than starting a church. Practices which worked to enable that, such as coaching groups, discipleship pods (cells) and one-to-one mentoring developed and grew.

One of the leaders interviewed raised questions about whether this was actually church. His intention was to eventually develop Christian communities of faith and he identified steps towards this, building on the discipleship groups which were in place.

It may be that in such a context any definition of church may need to be stretched. The other example was more readily identified as church, including discipleship groups alongside a service, albeit somewhat chaotic, which included time for worship, prayer, teaching and communion.

When working with people who have been marginalised by wider society and by the church, building up trust is crucial. One leader in referring to belonging, believing, behaving explained that asking people to belong to church first is inappropriate in this context. They start by 'blessing' which

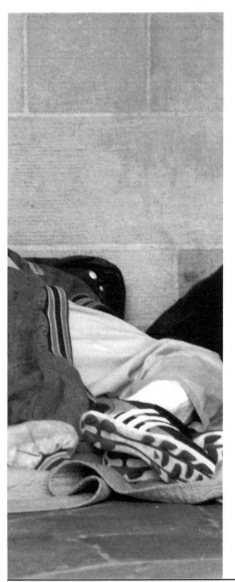

involves sharing God's love through practical help and often involves food. Through this they are able to get to know groups of young adults and over time demonstrate that they are trustworthy. Meeting together over food helps develop community, build trust and alongside this, coaching and discipleship happens.

Both the churches studied were based in Urban Priority Areas. They used public spaces such as parks, McDonald's and a YMCA to meet in. Neither group used church buildings, but one also used homes for discipleship groups.

Who are they reaching?

These churches were mainly reaching young adults from a non-churched background. At least 80% were from non-churched backgrounds and where there was some experience of church they often had been marginalised by the church so could be violently anti church. The young adults reached had high levels of poverty, illness, mental health, addictions, suicide, homelessness, violence and criminal activity.

Growth

On the subject of growth, the leaders talked about the importance of food, being a blessing, evangelism, inviting people along, and being welcoming.

Leaders talked about the slow process of growth in individuals, and the scale of pastoral issues in a community with high levels of poverty, addiction and mental health issues.

Both hoped for more Christians to help volunteer, disciple and lead.

One church had struggled when key volunteers moved on and highlighted the lack of mature Christians to lead and develop the church further. Being connected to the wider church at this point was crucial and helped them move through this vulnerable period.

5. Context shaped church

What are they like?

Whilst each of the churches in this research were aware of their context, the churches which were defined as context shaped churches developed and were intentionally shaped through direct interaction with their context.

They asked questions such as, 'What is the gospel here?' and 'What is church here?' Two churches were identified as contextual. One further church was transitioning towards being a context shaped church.

What do they do?

These churches were embedded into their specific context. Practices were markedly different between the contexts. However, each included times of gathering, without standard Sunday service features.

Gatherings were regular but would not necessarily happen weekly or on a Sunday. Whilst traditional elements of church, such as Eucharist, teaching, worship, prayer, discipleship and fellowship were evident, there was often no clear service, or preaching or singing.

Communion was administered, and all three churches had clergy or close links to clergy to enable this.

These churches had a range of connecting points through cafés, projects, and discussion groups, through which people could link up, get involved and explore faith.

The emphasis in these groups tended to be more on community and mission as starting places from which worship could develop.

> *"If you get the cultural environment right, community and discipleship just happens.*

These context shaped churches used a range of spaces with a mix of sacred and secular buildings, for example a café with chapel, the use of public city centre venues plus events in a cathedral. By using a range of spaces, these churches crossed the sacred/secular divide.

Where church planting hubs used sacred buildings for worship and secular spaces for evangelism, these context shaped churches used public spaces to develop community and share faith, alongside sacred spaces giving non-threatening opportunities for people to encounter God and grow in faith.

These churches, like the deconstructed churches, had a small church gathering of about 30 and a wider network or 100+ people attending events, projects or cafés. Overtly Christian gatherings tend to have a higher percentage of Christians with about 55% Christians from a churched background and 45% non-churched. However, of the wider network connected to the church, about 80% of them are from non-churched backgrounds.

Discipleship and leadership

Discipleship was happening often informally and on a one-to-one basis. Leaders talked about discipleship without becoming 'churchy'.

Developing leaders from those new to the faith was slow and sometimes a complicated process.

Who are they reaching?

Based in town or city centres, the churches in this study were generally reaching middle class students and postgraduates. One church was working in the alternative community and reaching people often excluded from church, although not marginalised by society at large.

Growth

In talking about reasons for growth, leaders cited evangelism, unashamed advertising, inviting people along, being welcoming, having good networkers within the context, being culturally embedded with approachable entry points, and non-threatening ways to encounter God without having to go to a church service.

One church found that succession issues hampered growth. Leaders moving on after a few years can be difficult for these fledgling communities. One of the churches interviewed found they struggled to sustain the church after the ordained pioneer moved on following their curacy. They found themselves overstretched and have recently taken the difficult decision to stop the work with young adults as they did not have the resources to sustain it.

Pastoral and discipleship issues were cited as factors which hampered growth. With a high percentage of people from non-Christian backgrounds and a smaller percentage of functional Christian young adults, developing leaders and teams was a complicated and slow process.

Being linked into wider church structures was important for all three churches, particularly in developing the sacramental life of the church and in supporting the church when leaders move on.

Wider issues

Gender

Encouragingly, gender figures in the young adult churches in this study bucked trends in the wider Church, where the average breakdown across denominations is 35% male and 65% female [6].

In **church planting hubs** (1) and **youth church grown up** (2) around 40% were male and 60% female. **Deconstructed churches** (3) had about 55% male and 45% female (some gender-specific work, which would inflate female numbers, is not included in this figure). **Churches on the margins** (4) were the reverse of (1) and (2) - 60% male and 40% female (some gender-specific work which would inflate male numbers is not included). **Context shaped churches** (5) were split roughly 50-50.

As this research is qualitative, numbers are not large enough to make conclusive remarks about gender in new forms of church, but the number of men in the churches studied is encouraging.

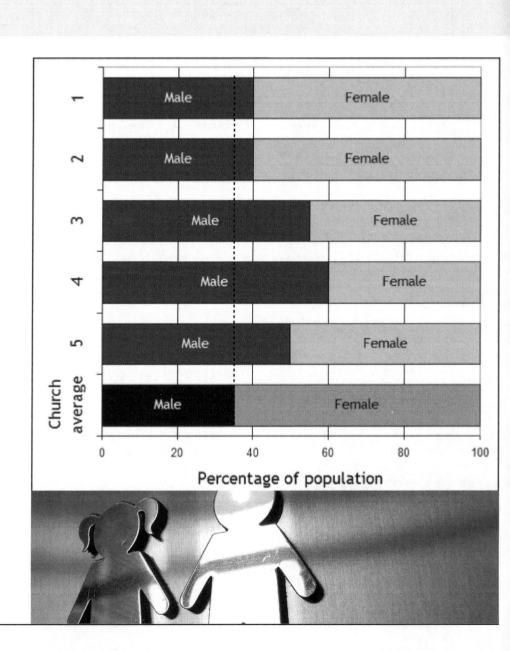

Ecclesial tradition

During this research it was difficult to find a range of ecclesial traditions fitting the criteria and happy to engage with the research. Most examples given are evangelical or charismatic, or came from that background. However, leaders did talk about a blending of traditions depending on context, drawing on the Church's rich history and range of practices. Those connecting with closed de-churched also talked of blending traditions along with a developing post-evangelical or post-church theology. The influence of monastic life and teaching was also evident.

There are a range of denominations present in the research, including Church of England, Methodist, Baptist, free churches with links into church planting networks, and those planted from acknowledged mission communities such as CMS and Church Army. Some were a mix of denominations, some were not officially linked to anything but do have relational links to other church organisations.

Just a life stage?

Questions remain over whether the traits and issues connected to young adults are cultural, or dependent on life stage. If they were life stage dependent we would expect to see young adults moving on in time into more traditional churches with a range of ages present. Although the research could not cover these questions adequately due the to ages of those studied, there was some evidence that those who had rejected church or had no prior experience of church were unlikely to transition into more traditional forms of church as they age, whereas young adults attending church planting hubs and youth churches that had grown up did move on to traditional family based churches. This could be into other congregations within the larger church, or into newly formed congregations connected to the larger church or other churches. Both these types of young adults' church had similar practices to the family based congregations they moved on to, shaped around a Sunday service alongside midweek discipleship groups and mission. However, those attending deconstructed, marginalised or context shaped churches may struggle to make the jump to more traditional forms of church. This suggests the determining factor is not their age or life stage, and that these new forms of church will grow and develop with their people.

The recognition of these small sacramental communities as church is vital, both for the sustainability of these fledgling churches and for the building up of the wider church. Issues remain about permissions, authorisation, and the appropriate administration of the sacraments, and all these need careful consideration. Some dioceses and some acknowledged mission communities are making strides in recognising, endorsing and supporting these churches.

Connection to the wider Church

The wider Church plays an important role in these churches. For those connected to larger churches, relationship to the wider Church happens primarily through their local larger church, with little direct link to the diocese. These local larger churches may benefit from the wisdom, gifts and theology present within acknowledged mission communities, such as Church Army or CMS, if they want to develop their mission and evangelism and reach further beyond the existing Church.

For those not in church planting hubs the wider Church has a significant role, especially in times of transition. Acknowledged mission communities, church planting networks and dioceses play a vital role here. Support (or lack of) can greatly affect the growth of churches. Leaders in marginalised and context shaped churches found being linked into wider Church structures very important, in particular when leaders moved on and in times of transition. Good relationships with the wider Church can be the difference between these young churches dying or continuing. This appears to work best when the relationship between the young adults' church and wider church exists and is strong before difficulties arise.

Deconstructed churches were least likely to be linked into the wider church, but benefited where they were. Also the use of town centre churches and cathedrals for events and gatherings was greatly appreciated.

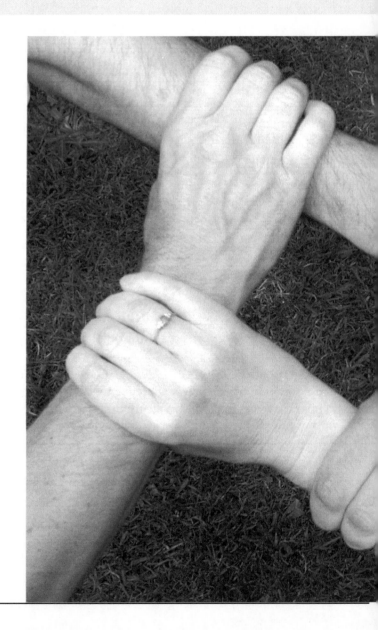

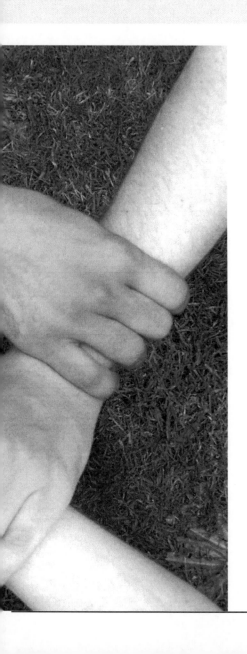

Leadership

Across all five types there was a wide range of leadership resource. Some had ordained leaders, others were led by lay evangelists and others by untrained lay volunteers. Some had full time employed leaders, others were self supporting, yet others were leading the church in their spare time.

It was significant and noteworthy that it was not the time, training, or the resource the leaders had which affected the development of the church, but the type of church which made the difference to its practices and growth. Where churches had employed leaders they experienced more acute succession problems. This has implications for the deployment of OPM curates, especially when this is also associated with access to a vicarage (see below). Where no one was employed, the leadership team felt the ongoing lack of resources. These churches found it especially difficult when core members moved on.

Size and sustainability

There was a distinct difference between larger churches attracting Christian young adults and smaller churches reaching those with no previous church experience, or those who had rejected church. Those larger young adults' congregations exist in close relationship to larger churches, having access to their resources and draw their model of sustainability and accountability.

The smaller churches whilst reaching a much larger network often form a core group of about thirty people and meet in buildings which accommodate community meals. The use of community houses or vicarages is important in the life of these small Christian communities. However, young adults often do not own homes which are large enough for this. The provision of buildings for this is one way a diocese can support the development of a new young adults' church.

Conclusion

This research provides evidence that some churches are reaching, retaining and discipling young adults from a range of socio-economic and religious backgrounds.

Five distinct types of young adults' church have been identified, with each type connecting with different kinds of young adults and practicing faith in different ways. Those reaching Christians or those on the fringe of church exhibit more traditional church practices, whilst those working further away from the existing church develop more experimental and contextual practices.

The marked similarities amongst church planting hubs and youth churches grown up, in contrast to the similarities found amongst deconstructed, marginalised and context shaped churches, suggest that young adults with no previous church experience are unlikely to attend a church organised around a Sunday service, however contemporary in style.

Conversely churches embodying transformational and sacramental community which are embedded within their context, though small and more vulnerable than the larger young adult churches, do connect with young adults from a broader religious and socio-economic background.

Whilst the growth of these young adults' churches is encouraging, the number of young adults attending church remains worryingly low compared to the overall population of young adults.

The church can respond to this by encouraging the variety of expressions of churches reaching young adults and releasing resources, such as empty vicarages, to these fledgling communities.

Supportive and positive links to the wider church should be encouraged and consideration given to how these communities can develop their sacramental life further.

Appendix 1: research subjects

Andy Croft	Soul Survivor Watford	Watford
Bryony Wells	Life Church, St Thomas' Church Crookes	Sheffield
Harry Steele	Uncut (part of All Saints Ecclesall), then St Peter's, Greenhill	Sheffield
Mark Broomhead	Order of the Black Sheep	Chesterfield
Rich Atkinson	Rebuilding Generation, St Toms, Philadelphia	Sheffield
Shannon Hopkins	Matryoshka Haus	London
Steve Leach	Un-named group, plus Church for the Night	Bournemouth
Carol Wain	11.57	Liverpool
James Henley	The Lab	Newport
Nick Russell	Church Army Centre of Mission	Greenwich
Sarah Belcher	Monks Road Congregation, Threshold	Lincoln
Steve Clarke	FEIG	Gloucester

Fresh Expressions young adults round table

The Fresh Expressions young adults round table draws together organisations and individuals working with young adults to share knowledge, develop best practice and support those pioneering fresh expressions for young adults.
freshexpressions.org.uk/roundtables

Take it further

The Fresh Expressions *mission shaped ministry* course is a one-year, part-time course equipping participants to plant and sustain fresh expressions of church.
freshexpressions.org.uk/missionshapedministry

ReSource weekends allow you to meet people who are doing mission in diverse contexts, hear their stories, hang out with their communities and think about what you can learn for your own context. You can dive into one weekend or do all four in a year to get a much broader experience.
resourcemission.com

Share booklets combine spiritual insight with practical knowledge to offer guidance in starting and sustaining a fresh expression of church.
freshexpressions.org.uk/share/booklets

The Guide is an online guide for all involved with fresh expressions of church - practitioners, people in training, encouragers, supporters and researchers.
freshexpressions.org.uk/guide

Further resources including reading lists and related publications can be found on the Fresh Expressions website.

freshexpressions.org.uk/resources

Published 2013 by Fresh Expressions
Registered charity #1080103

Copyright © Fresh Expressions 2013
freshexpressions.org.uk

Author: Beth Keith
Designer: Ben Clymo

ISBN: 978-0-9560005-7-6